A More Desirable Way

Leadership with the one true King

Exploring a Jesus-centred
team leadership model

Bruno Loyiso

ShareOne Publishings.

A More Desirable Way - Leadership with the one true King
Copyright © 2020 by Bruno Loyiso Guntelach and ShareOne® Publishings

Credit to the first and second editor, Veronika Gloeck and Lauren Phillips.
Cover Design: Junio Rodrigues

All rights reserved. No part of this book may be reproduced in any form without permission in writing from the publisher and author.

Unless otherwise indicated, all Scripture quotations are taken from the *Holy Bible*, New Living Translation, copyright © 1996, 2004, 2015 by Tyndale House Foundation. Used by permission of Tyndale House Publishers, Inc., Carol Stream, Illinois 60188. All rights reserved.

Scripture quotations labeled NIV are from The Holy Bible, New International Version®, NIV® Copyright © 1973, 1978, 1984, 2011 by Biblica, Inc.® Used by permission. All rights reserved worldwide.

Scripture quotations marked MSG are taken from *THE MESSAGE*, copyright © 1993, 2002, 2018 by Eugene H. Peterson. Used by permission of NavPress. All rights reserved. Represented by Tyndale House Publishers, Inc.

Concordance quotations marked Strong's Concordance are taken from Strong's Exhaustive Concordance: New American Standard Bible. Updated ed. La Habra: Lockman Foundation, 1995.
http://www.biblestudytools.com/concordancestrongs-exhaustive-concordance/

First published in 2020 by ShareOne® Publishings
ISBN Softcover: 978-3-907312-00-1
ISBN Hardcover: 978-3-907312-03-2
eISBN (ebook): 978-3-907312-01-8
eISBN (pdf): 978-3-907312-02-5

To all the leaders out there, who, like Moses (and I), are tired of carrying the burden of leadership alone.

Table of Content

Endorsements 6

Inception 9

In The Beginning 15

The Steering Wheel 24

Caring Leadership 32

Who's Our Centre? 38

A Sneak Peek 46

The Setback 55

Conflict Resolution 62

Common Questions 71

A More Desirable Way 86

The Crown 90

ShareOne® 91

Pay What Feels Right 93

Acknowledgments 94

About The Author 96

Endorsements

I have known Bruno and his family for the last ten years. The book that you are about to read, "A More Desirable Way", is not fiction; it is a true story of a personal journey and I have had the privilege of witnessing this story as it unfolded.

I would recommend any person aspiring to be a leader, as well as anyone leading a multicultural organisation, to have this book by their side.

Wilson Goeda, former National Director of YWAM South Africa and author of the book "Why Me?"

—

Through my personal experience, after having finished extensive studies in Theology and Missiology and served almost 50 years in full time ministry - many years as the Field Director of YWAM Africa and also in various other leadership roles, I have come to the conclusion that leadership should be an ever evolving dynamic that embraces different cultures and contexts. Leadership should continue to adapt, and this book presents key insights into a leadership approach that is relevant for the future. In his captivating book, Bruno challenges old ideas and presents a leadership approach that promotes expansion and can be adapted to various contexts and cultures.

I have seen Bruno live out the principles described in this book, and it is with deep appreciation for his service in YWAM, that I commend this book to you.

Kobus van Niekerk, former Field Director of YWAM Africa

—

Bruno's book has impacted my life powerfully. My spirit has longed for "A More Desirable Way" of leadership for a long time.

At the very moment when I was prompted to re-embark on pulling a ministry team together in our region in France, God put me in touch with Bruno!

I was so relieved, comforted and inspired by his journey. God is doing amazing things amongst us as we now dare to put Jesus back in the centre of our team.

Thank you Bruno, and the YWAM Worcester team.

Sarah Paine, wife, mother, artist, art-therapist, children's worker, co-pioneer of house church movements

—

I have known Bruno since 2000 when, as a young man, he came from Switzerland to do his Discipleship Training School at YWAM Worcester, where I was leading the Base.

Endorsements

I have always admired Bruno for his willingness to learn, and his ability to glean the most out of his experiences.

This book is case in point. Bruno applied Biblical principles to the challenges he faced as a leader while also navigating the shift in leadership approach that started to emerge in YWAM and other organisations around the world. His experiences and insights are distilled in this book.

I believe this book will be a helpful resource for leaders seeking to transition into team leadership.

Stefaan Hugo, International speaker and former Regional Director of YWAM Southern Africa and Indian Ocean Islands

—

In Ephesians 1:23 we read that the church is not only Christ's body, but is also described as the fullness of Him who fills all in all. This is an exalted description, indeed, but it is not given to any individual. This belongs to the body corporately and only in the body can such fullness be found. Bruno's book describes a leadership style that can draw on the whole body and therefore on the richness of this passage. Please read this book with a prayerful attitude and ponder how you can lead in such a way as to reap from the riches of everyone's anointing, insight, understanding, and ability.

Jim Stier, former President of YWAM international, founder of YWAM Brazil, author of the book "The Way of Faith"

Chapter 1

Inception

Although I am a man with the common desire of being significant, appreciated and affirmed, I never aspired to become the leader of a large organisation. I was happy with things as they were. I had leadership roles in smaller teams and I was even part of the leadership team of Youth With A Mission (YWAM) Worcester in South Africa; a team with a strong leader who gave us all security. This leader was interested in our contributions and included us in the decision making process, but he was ultimately still the one who would make all the tough calls.

There wasn't much need for us as team members to step up, which was a comfortable place to be. I was able to flourish in my strategic, influencing and relational strengths, and while I did take up various responsibilities and even managed to help the organisation get out of debt, there was no real risk involved for me as I wasn't the one who had to carry the final responsibility. No, that final say was not for me to carry, but for our strong leader. And he did.

This said leader was a good leader: spirit-filled, apostolic with a great understanding of the big picture and the ability to see the details; a leader with a clear vision and with the strengths to lead us all towards it. He was the leader who re-pioneered the work of YWAM Worcester between 1998 and 2010 at its new location in town. He started with about 12 people on his pioneering team and built the Base to a recognisable size of about 120 volunteers; a number of solid community development projects; as well as approximately 300 students per year. He had a special gift of drawing and uniting people from all over the globe, and we consistently had more than 30 different nations represented on our Worcester base.

For me the world was completely in order and comfortable. The ways in which I got involved were energizing and fulfilling. I enjoyed everything I was doing and had one of the best times of my life. I never struggled to get up in the mornings, as I always had something to look forward to.

> **For me the world was completely in order and comfortable.**

So, when I was requested to prayerfully consider taking on the overall leadership of YWAM Worcester, my initial response was one of laughter. I had no intention whatsoever to change anything about my so-called perfect life. I said, "I will pray about it, but I don't think this is the right thing for me."

Well, I did pray, and in doing so, I underwent an uncomfortable time of processing with the Lord, my wife, my leaders, some friends and my elders. And the Lord spoke! How He spoke is enough material for another book. But let me assure you of this: Never in my life have I heard Him more clearly and with more external confirmations as I did then.

It became absolutely evident that God wanted me to accept the appointment of leading YWAM Worcester into the next season. And so it came to pass that in September 2010, I was inaugurated as the new leader of YWAM Worcester in South Africa. This, of course, was a great privilege and it was generally well received by those involved. What followed was a beautiful time of transition: the previous leader and his family remained in Worcester for a few more years, and because we had a strong, trusting relationship, it became a wonderful testimony of how he lit my torch, rather than him handing over his baton and leaving. In fact I grew a lot in my own leadership capacity by meeting with him regularly and receiving valuable advice, whenever I asked for it.

What I didn't know at the time of my inauguration was the struggles and trials that were awaiting me and my leadership team, and how vital it would become for me to know that God had clearly called me into this leadership responsibility. If I didn't have such a clear word from the Lord, together with the confirmations that accompanied it, I would not even have endured the first seven months of my leadership assignment. Gone were the perfect days where everything I did was energising and fulfilling, where getting up in the mornings was a celebration of what was about to come in that new day.

> **Gone were the perfect days where everything I did was energising and fulfilling.**

Fraud, deception and theft, violence between students, and fatal accidents were some of the issues we had to handle during the first seven months of my leadership, and in the years to come. These were very difficult situations to deal with, especially since none of us on the leadership team were prepared, trained nor qualified to navigate these turbulent waters. But God sent us great help through the guidance of trusted advisors and counsellors. The elders of our Region supported us on many levels, and by connecting with God in prayer we received Divine wisdom when we needed it most. We surely grew a lot as we faced each challenge. We learned remarkable lessons about crisis management, but more importantly we unknowingly learned some foundational principles of team leadership. And while we weren't fully functioning as a team yet, vital pillars were being built which ultimately led us into a graceful process of exploring and discovering a Biblical model of Jesus-centred team leadership.

While I'm not claiming to be an expert in this field, I do hope that this book will be a helpful contribution in your own process of discovering "A More Desirable Way" of leadership: A

Inception   13

relational type of leadership that has no need for any other king but the one true King.

May this book invite you to evaluate the cultural leadership model with which you've grown up. May it stir up fruitful discussions and inspire you to engage with a Biblical leadership model that is not often taught in mainstream leadership seminars. And, may it lead you on a rich and beautiful journey with Jesus where you would find encouragement and inspiration from Him.

While I'm sharing my personal experience, gleaned from the journey YWAM Worcester is in the midst of, we ourselves have not arrived at the destination of perfectly implementing Jesus-centred team leadership, and quite frankly, the destination should not be our goal. Rather, we are making daily, sometimes imperfect, choices to place Jesus at the centre, while trusting the diverse giftings of a team to lead our organisation into the future. Leading with the one true King is an ongoing journey, one where we can always discover more of Him and grow in our relationship with Him. And this is what really matters.

> **Leading with the one true King is an ongoing journey.**

May the story of our successes and setbacks encourage you in your own daily choices - not necessarily to reach a destination, but rather to take the next step, in your context, towards leading with Jesus as the one true King.

Since we ourselves are still discovering more of the wealth of this leadership approach, I simply invite you to join us on an expedition of observing, wrestling and discerning.

> And by His grace,
> may God crown us
> with fresh Divine Revelation along the way.

Chapter 2

In The Beginning

Genesis 1
1 In the beginning God created the heavens and the earth...

...26 Then God said, "Let us make human beings in our image, to be like us. They will reign over the fish in the sea, the birds in the sky, the livestock, all the wild animals on the earth, and the small animals that scurry along the ground." 27 So God created human beings in his own image. In the image of God he created them; male and female he created them. 28 Then God blessed them and said, "Be fruitful and multiply. Fill the earth and govern it. Reign over the fish in the sea, the birds in the sky, and all the animals that scurry along the ground."

God - Father, Son and Holy Spirit - three in one, who said to Himself "let us...", is the ultimate model of fellowship, team, family and unity. Together the Trinity created. God's very identity portrays an interdependence between the Persons of the Godhead and this same interdependence was transferred to us when God created us in His image.

We were created for the same communion with Him and with others. When God commissioned mankind to govern the earth and reign over His creation, He did so with the intention that we would govern and reign from a place of intimate relationship with Him and with those around us.

Sadly, it didn't take long for mankind to reject God's original design. We were created in His image, but failed to embrace the interdependence that this entailed. Instead we succumbed to the deceptive suggestion of the serpent to disobey God by eating from the forbidden fruit, so that we would *"...be like God, knowing both good and evil."* (Genesis 3:5b).

Instead of trusting God, in whose image we were created, we turned our back and pursued the exact opposite of our destiny: We separated ourselves from Him. When Adam and Eve heard God walking around in the garden, they *"...hid from the Lord God among the trees."* (Genesis 3:8b), while He, the God who embodies the desire for relationship *"... called to the man: 'Where are you?'"* (Genesis 3:9).

Throughout Biblical history we observe that God was always seeking fellowship with His people. He cannot but be relational, as this is who He is!

> **He cannot but be relational, as this is who He is!**

In Genesis 18, we read about how the Lord appeared to Abraham as *"three men"* (verse 2). He (represented by the three men) promised Abraham and Sarah that at about the same time the following year, they would have a son (verse 10). When the men left and looked toward Sodom, God (personified in the three men) had a conversation with Himself asking, *"Should I hide my plan from Abraham?"* (verse 17). What follows, is a rather interesting discussion. Now let's first clarify this fact: The Bible does not say that God told Abraham He was planning on destroying Sodom and Gomorrah, as is often believed. All He said was that He had heard about the flagrant sin of these two cities and that *"...I am going down to see if their actions are as wicked as I have heard. If not, I want to know."* (verse 21).

It's at this point that Abraham approached the approachable God, and asked Him a few "what if" questions. God was perfectly fine with Abraham's questions. In fact it seems to me that God actually enjoyed Abraham's participation, as he was behaving himself exactly in the way he was created to: In God's image and for relationship.

"In His image?" you may ask.

Yes, I believe that Abraham reflected the character of God when he relationally engaged with God and asked:

23 ... "Will you sweep away both the righteous and the wicked? 24 Suppose you find fifty righteous people living there in the city—will you still sweep it away and not spare it for their sakes? 25 Surely you wouldn't do such a thing, destroying the righteous along with the wicked. Why, you would be treating the righteous and the wicked exactly the same! Surely you wouldn't do that! Should not the Judge of all the earth do what is right?" (Genesis 18:23-25).

And I see this confirmed by God's response:

26 ... "If I find fifty righteous people in Sodom, I will spare the entire city for their sake." (Genesis 18:26).

And the conversation continued in a similar way in the following verses. Every time Abraham suggested that God shouldn't destroy the righteous, God confirmed that He indeed wouldn't. I believe that God was proud of Abraham, because he demonstrated the likeness of God by pointing out Divine righteousness and by practicing intimacy with God.

But now, let us look at the Israelites. God appointed Moses to lead the Israelites out of Egypt (Exodus 3:10). From this point on, Moses was in such frequent contact with God that he doubtlessly had an extraordinary relationship with Him. Later, in the desert at Mount Sinai when God wanted to speak to the Israelites directly without Moses having to be the intermediary (Exodus 20), the people were so scared of God that they pleaded for Moses to speak to God on their behalf: *"And they said to Moses, 'You speak to us, and we will listen. But don't let God speak directly to us, or we will die!'"* (Exodus 20:19).

> **You speak to us, and we will listen. But don't let God speak directly to us, or we will die!**

Here we see that God had a desire to interact directly with the people as He had created them in His image and for relationship. The people, on the other hand, were afraid of God and preferred Moses to be their advocate so they wouldn't have to engage with God themselves.

Later on in the Biblical narrative, in 1 Samuel 8, we read about how the elders of Israel demanded Samuel: *"Give us a king to judge us like all the other nations have."* (1 Samuel 8:5b). Samuel was displeased with their request and went to the Lord for guidance, to which God responded: *"7 Do everything they say to you, for they are rejecting me, not you. They don't want me to be their king any longer. 8 Ever since I brought them from Egypt they have continually abandoned me and followed other gods. And now they are giving you the same treatment. 9 Do as they ask, but solemnly warn them about the way a king will reign over them."* (1 Samuel 8:7-9).

This response makes it clear that God never intended for Israel to have a king other than Himself. He, the one true King, wanted to be their king! But Israel rejected Him and wanted to have a human king *"like other nations have"*. Despite the fact that God had Samuel warn the Israelites about how different and harmful a human king would be for them, they still chose to replicate the model of leadership they observed in the nations around them.

> **He, the one true King, wanted to be their king!**

God wants a relationship with us. He wants to be our King. He doesn't see the need for us to have a king between Himself and us. His reign is vastly different from the reign of any human king. Human kings fail. God never fails. Human kings always harbour a degree of selfishness. God cannot be selfish.

In 1 John 4 we read that *"God is love"* (agape). We understand from this that God's very character is an extravagantly loving one. What then would it look like if God were to reign in our teams? It certainly would look very different from human reign! Let us explore the type of fruit we could expect to see if the loving God was to reign and lead.

Galatians 5 explains to us what *"the fruit of the Spirit"* is. Some reputable theologians interpret this passage in a way that really appeals to me. They say that since the passage mentions fruit (singular), it can be assumed that the fruit of the Spirit is the first mentioned *"love"* (agape), and that the eight adjectives that follow are describing the characteristics of that fruit (agape), namely: *"joy, peace, patience, kindness, goodness, faithfulness, gentleness, and self-control."* This interpretation resonates with me and I feel that 1 Corinthians 13 potentially confirms this view as it describes love (agape) in similar terms, using a few more words:

> *"4 Love is patient and kind. Love is not jealous or boastful or proud 5 or rude. It does not demand its own way. It is not irritable, and it keeps*

no record of being wronged. 6 It does not rejoice about injustice but rejoices whenever the truth wins out. 7 Love never gives up, never loses faith, is always hopeful, and endures through every circumstance."
(1 Corinthians 13:4-7).

So in summary: One of God's strongest attributes or characteristics is love (agape). The qualities of love (agape) according to Galatians 5 and 1 Corinthians 13 are: Joy, peace, patience, kindness, goodness, faithfulness, gentleness and self-control. Love is not jealous, boastful, proud or rude. It doesn't demand its own way, is not irritable and keeps no record of being wronged. It stands for truth rather than injustice, never gives up, never loses faith, always is hopeful and endures through every circumstance.

Now, how would you like a king with these qualities?

Well, God is exactly that kind of King. He is the one true King and His character manifests unconditional love (agape). And because of that, God gives us the choice of whether or not we want Him as our King. He will never force us into being His subjects. And even when we choose Him as our King, we will never merely be subjects to Him, but co-rulers (Genesis 1:28). He longs for us to choose Him, because He knows that it is in our own best interest to do so. We do not need a mediator. We do not need someone who stands in between us and God. We can relate and commune directly with Him. We can learn to hear His voice and follow Him without an intermediary leader telling us what to do.

> **He** is the one true King and His character manifests unconditional love (agape).

In John 10 we read:
14 "I am the good shepherd; I know my own sheep, and they know me, 15 just as my Father knows me and I know the Father. So I sacrifice my life for the sheep... 27 My sheep listen to my voice; I know them, and they follow me." (John 10:14-15,27)

The Good Shepherd knows us, and we can know Him too. If we do, we will listen to Him and follow Him. It means direct relationship with the King. It means fellowship, conversations, discussions, co-creating and co-ruling with Him.

Now, I'm not suggesting that there should be no leadership other than God. Throughout history, God has appointed leadership. But Divine leadership looks very different to the leadership that has commonly been modelled to us and it is vastly different to our cultural understanding of leadership. The kind of leadership I'd like to introduce to you doesn't manifest itself in the role of a mediator between God and men. Instead it points, directs and gently nudges its followers towards God, encouraging them to hear His voice for themselves. At the same time, it doesn't abandon its followers to their own devices and leave them on their own. Rather it provides support, discipleship and facilitates growth. It seeks to empower others and requires a lot of self-sacrifice.

This is the kind of leadership we are being invited to explore. After all, we are created in the image of God, the one true King. And although we have fallen away from that very image, through Christ we can be restored back to it, as it says in 2 Corinthians 3:

18 And we all, who with unveiled faces contemplate the Lord's glory, are being transformed into his image with ever-increasing glory, which comes from the Lord, who is the Spirit.
(2 Corinthians 3:18 - NIV).

> **After all, we are created in the image of God, the one true King.**

"Contemplating the Lord's glory" means spending time with Him, getting to know Him more and surrounding ourselves with Him. And as we do that, this passage predicts that we will be restored back into His image. But this is not a quick, instant kind of transformation. The text is written in the continuous present tense, which indicates that it's a process that is happening on an ongoing basis and will take time.

So as we fellowship with God, His presence starts a process of transforming us. An ongoing process that is restoring us back into His image. And as we are being transformed, we are also being empowered to lead more and more in the way He does.

Chapter 3

The Steering Wheel

One thing that I realised early on in my leadership was that I wasn't going to be able to be a strong and charismatic leader as my predecessor was. As I processed this with my father-in-law he gave me vital advice, which today I call the Jetroic concept, because it was Jetro, Moses' father-in-law, who advised Moses of almost the exact same thing, just on a larger scale. (see Exodus 18). Basically, I was advised to put a stronger emphasis on team leadership and in doing so, to split all the major responsibilities into different departments. I was then to empower the department heads to run each of these departments, make decisions and take up responsibility within the scope of their department, rather than trying to be a strong leader who administered everything myself. Simple advice which immediately made sense to me. However, I understood that the implementation of this advice would require a significant change of culture in our Organisation, with regard to how we did leadership. And I knew from previous experience that changing a culture was going to take time, wisdom, patience and perseverance.

Shortly after my inauguration as the YWAM Worcester leader, someone said to me: "Always remember that changing the course of an organisation can be compared to changing the course of a large ship like the Titanic. You can turn the steering wheel in an instant, but the ship will be slow to follow." This picture certainly helped me in the years to come.

> **You turn the steering wheel in an instant, but the ship will be slow to follow.**

Although the process was not always easy, and we did initially face some resistance, it was very freeing when the department heads started to take responsibility. Not just for me, as the overall leader, but also for the department heads themselves, as they were given authority and felt empowered. While the department heads had decision making power and used it to the best of their ability, we also tried to model "inter-dependence" as opposed to "independence". We didn't want to make independent decisions, but rather aimed to depend on one another in our decision making, through building stronger relationships and processing issues together well, sometimes maybe even too extensively.

But in all of this, I always felt that something was missing. Something I couldn't really pin down yet, but I knew that if we could find this missing link, then the way we led would change and potentially bear much more fruit.

On a beautiful sunny day in September 2013, I was walking our dogs in the unique scenery of the South African Karoo "veld" (field), when I received a phone call from my predecessor, my Spiritual Father. He explained to me that YWAM had started a process of adjusting their leadership structure internationally. YWAM had decided to move away from a business type structure - with directors, presidents and chairmen - back to a family type structure - with fathers, mothers, grandparents and/or elders.

And so, our YWAM Global leadership laid down their titles and over the course of the following years our Regional and National leaders did the same. YWAM was reorganised into different Areas and Area Circle Teams were introduced to convene these Areas in a family type of way.

It was always emphasised that this structural change was primarily intended for the National, Regional and Global leadership, while on a local base level, we would still need directors to maintain legal accountability. That said, when I heard about this structural adjustment for the first time, my spirit was filled with excitement. There was something about this concept that resonated with me. Could this be the missing link that I wasn't able to pin down when it came to our Worcester base leadership?

So, very inspired, I brought this to the attention of our leadership team and suggested that we consider this model for our local base context too. I proposed that I would step down as the director and instead we would have a team of elders leading together, much like the apostles led the early church. However, the leadership team wasn't quite ready at the time, and they suggested that instead of me stepping down, they would all step up and take on more responsibility. Well, I did want them to step up, so I agreed.

A few months later our leadership team made a key decision to go on a retreat to hear from the Lord with regard to this matter. We assumed that if the Lord could speak to the global body of our Mission about this change in leadership structure, He surely could also have a personal word for us as a local base. And so we spent some time in prayer, asking the Lord for a personalised word for us at YWAM Worcester. And lo and behold, He spoke. Three of us received, independently from each other, the passage in Acts 6:1-7 where it says:

"But as the believers rapidly multiplied, there were rumblings of discontent. The Greek-speaking believers complained about the Hebrew-speaking believers, saying that their widows were being discriminated against in the daily distribution of food.
2 So the Twelve called a meeting of all the believers. They said, 'We apostles should spend our time teaching the word of God, not running a food program. 3 And so, brothers, select seven men who are well respected and are full of the Spirit and wisdom. We will give them this responsibility. 4 Then we apostles can spend our time in prayer and teaching the word.'
5 Everyone liked this idea, and they chose the following: Stephen (a man full of faith and the Holy Spirit), Philip, Procorus, Nicanor,

Timon, Parmenas, and Nicolas of Antioch (an earlier convert to the Jewish faith). 6 These seven were presented to the apostles, who prayed for them as they laid their hands on them.
7 So God's message continued to spread. The number of believers greatly increased in Jerusalem, and many of the Jewish priests were converted, too." (Acts 6:1-7).

So here we got our personal word from the Lord. And it was very relevant to our situation. Our leadership team was so busy with all the daily management issues, that we found ourselves having little time for prayer and teaching the Word, which really should have been our primary focus. We had become a management team instead of a spiritual leadership team. We realised that we needed to change something significantly, but we only had partial understanding with regard to how and what needed to change. We understood that people needed to be empowered to step up and lead in the more practical issues of the Base, and that this would free us up for spiritual leadership, which was genuinely needed. And so, what followed was an extended season of changing our Base's structure. We interpreted the Acts 6 Scripture with the understanding we had at the time and implemented some significant changes. But ultimately we didn't quite yet succeed.

> **We had become a management team instead of a spiritual leadership team.**

We were in the process of learning. We certainly made a lot of mistakes and had to regularly adjust our processes. The fact that we were leading such a multicultural community didn't make it any easier. Many different cultures living and working together led to misunderstandings, misinterpretations, rivalries and hurts. What should have kept me on my knees asking the Lord for His wisdom and help, drove me into a season of trying and working harder. My hours extended more and more, my family life suffered extensively, and I didn't even know what the words "spare time" meant anymore. I set myself up for burnout, which I eventually was medically diagnosed with in 2016. This led me into a sabbatical time, during which I handed the leadership over to the team. I stayed at home for four months, focusing on the Lord, processing with my mentors and recharging by just having time to do what I really enjoyed.

One morning during my sabbatical, as I was opening the window of our bedroom to let some fresh air in, God whispered into my heart: "If you went back to work and found out that they didn't need you as their leader anymore, would you be delighted or offended?" I stood at the open window thinking deeply about that question. "Hmmm," I eventually answered back to Him, "I don't know. Probably both." Although this was the end of our conversation, I continued to process this question and my response to it. I was reminded of the time when I was walking my dogs and received that phone call informing me about the leadership structure change in YWAM globally. I remembered my initial response of excitement and how I had discerned that this could be "it" for us as a Base. I remembered how I then took the idea to our leadership team, proposing that I step down as the overall leader, so that we could lead together as a team of equals. I recalled how the team wasn't quite ready for such a step, but how I had continued to hope and pray that one day we would be able to dare that step.

> **If you went back to work and found out that they didn't need you as their leader anymore, would you be delighted or offended?**

I started realising that despite this desire to fully step into team leadership, I did enjoy the benefits of being the leader, being in power and having the final word. It had become comfortable. I was on a mission to change the direction of a large ship, by changing the way we do leadership, but I was still the one holding the steering wheel in my hands. Although I allowed the leadership team to help me turn this heavy steering wheel, I was still the one in charge, the weight of which ultimately led to my burnout. Something had to change, and that something had to be me.

Once I realised my need for change, God led me to the story of Moses in Numbers 11. I discovered that Moses had also experienced burnout. Although he had followed his father-in-law's advice of getting a team around him who would take up some of his responsibilities, he too still held onto the steering wheel. At some point Moses even became suicidal, asking the Lord to take his life since he could no longer bear the quarrelling and complaints of the Israelites. Moses was done with these people and just wanted to die. But the Lord responded to Moses:

16 "Gather before me seventy men who are recognised as elders and leaders of Israel. Bring them to the Tabernacle to stand there with you. 17 I will come down and talk to you there. I will take some of the Spirit that is upon you, and I will put the Spirit upon them also. They will bear the burden of the people along with you, so you will not have to carry it alone." (Numbers 11:16-17).

When I read this story I knew in my heart that I was prepared to go all the way now. I was going to hand the steering wheel over to God. I was going to trust Him that He would lead us as a Base and that He would take some of the Spirit that was upon me, and put the Spirit upon the team also. (see Numbers 11:17).

> **I was going to hand the steering wheel over to God.**

But would the team now be ready for this step? And what about the other staff on our Base?

Chapter 4

Caring Leadership

When I quoted the passage from the Book of Acts 6:1-7 in the previous chapter, I mentioned that as a team we interpreted this portion of Scripture with the limited understanding we had at the time, and that this led us to implementing some significant changes, which didn't ultimately succeed. Nevertheless, as we tried to navigate our way through these changes, we also discovered more and more of the treasures hidden in this Biblical story.

Now by no means do I claim, nor even believe, that I've received full revelation of Acts 6:1-7, but over the past few years I have grown into a much deeper understanding of this passage and its wealth. In this chapter, I'd like to take you with me on a journey through some of these fresh insights. You might want to go back to the previous chapter, or open your own Bible (Acts 6:1-7), to recap the details of the story.

The team of apostles had a problem. They knew what their main calling was (prayer and teaching the word of God), but they caught themselves reacting to the needs and demands of the people they were leading. There were issues, and these issues were real. Food needed to be distributed and it needed to be done in a just way. As the number of believers grew, so did the workload, which led to the Greek-speaking believers feeling disadvantaged in comparison to the Hebrew-speaking believers, causing them to complain. The apostles didn't present any excuses nor did they try to justify themselves. Instead they realised that these justice issues were distracting them from their main calling. And while these issues needed to be handled well, the apostles discerned that it was not for them to manage.

This is an example of great leadership. Mature leaders know their calling and stay focused, and when necessary they make adjustments to refocus. It is easy to get distracted by important issues. But the fact that the issues are important doesn't mean we should allow them to interfere with what we are called to do. As leaders we often feel a subtle expectation that if we don't take care of an issue ourselves, then we are not good and caring leaders.

> **As leaders we often feel a subtle expectation that if we don't take care of an issue ourselves, then we are not good and caring leaders.**

Well, this example in Acts 6 shows us that exactly the opposite is true: While the apostles took care of the matter themselves, injustice and favouritism was being perceived. It was only when the apostles took their hands off the issue and handed it over to a different group of leaders, who were specifically commissioned and anointed for this task, that the believers started to feel cared for again. Isn't this interesting? It's not by solving issues ourselves that we show care as leaders, rather it's by staying out of situations that are not supposed to distract us and instead handing these over to a specialised team, whose purpose it is to lead and care through these issues. And that's when people all of a sudden feel cared for again.

Most leaders, I know, do care for their people, and the leadership team of YWAM Worcester is no exception. But because we wanted to show our care, too often we got involved in issues that were not really for us to solve, as they were interfering with our primary purpose. Of course, what makes this even more difficult is the fact that whenever people feel mistreated or disadvantaged, they start complaining, expecting leadership to solve issues on their behalf. As leaders we are often tempted to submit to these expectations instead of leading, hoping to prove that we are good and caring leaders. Consequently, we get involved in issues that are not ours to solve. This, however, often leads to an even bigger mess and leaves people feeling even more disadvantaged and less cared for.

So what the apostles did was simply grand. They showed real care. Not by getting involved themselves, but by handing these specific issues over into competent hands.

> **They showed real care. Not by getting involved themselves, but by handing theses specific issues over into competent hands.**

At the same time, the apostles demonstrated that the calling to lead in practical issues was in no way less spiritual than their own leadership calling, which was *"prayer and teaching the word of God"*. (Acts 6:2). One of the ways we can see this is by looking at the criteria which the apostles required for this new leadership responsibility:

The appointed men had to be "well respected and full of the Spirit and wisdom". (Acts 6:3). The apostles didn't differentiate between "spiritual" and "practical" responsibilities. Instead their understanding was that we are all to be filled with the Spirit in order to live out our unique calling.

Another important detail is the fact that the men weren't selected by the apostles, but by the larger body of believers. As leaders we tend to think that we know best who should be chosen to lead. But in using this approach we end up appointing managers, not leaders. A leader is someone who has followers. So it is the followers who choose the person whom they entrust leadership to. The apostles understood this and so they had the "brothers" select the leaders who were to be appointed and given responsibility. Again, they did not choose just anyone, but "men who are well respected and are full of the Spirit and wisdom". (Acts 6:3).

Another principle that I find important to point out here is this: Although the larger body of believers selected the leaders according to the criteria laid out by the apostles, they did not do so outside of an accountable relationship with the apostles. Towards the end of the passage we read, *"these seven were presented to the apostles, who prayed for them as they laid their hands on them".* (Acts 6:6). Thus the larger body of believers chose their own leaders and then the apostles confirmed and approved of them by anointing them. There was mutual accountability and therefore mutual protection.

Another point that stands out for me is the fact that all this was done in a team context. Nowhere is it mentioned that the apostles were led by a single leader who had the final say over this matter. It was the team of apostles, the Twelve, who called the meeting of all believers. (Acts 6:2). It was the same Twelve who then anointed the seven men together. (Acts 6:6). Also, the apostles didn't ask the believers to choose one leader over them, they were encouraged to *"select seven men".* (Acts 6:3). And later, when the seven selected men were mentioned by name (Acts 6:5), none of them was singled out as the leader over the other six. Team was being modelled on all levels. Team without an overall leader - but not team without leadership. There is a difference and we will still get to discover more about this kind of team leadership later in this book.

Team was being modelled on all levels. Team without an overall leader.

Now, would you like to see what the outcome was of this caring, accountable and relational team leadership as demonstrated by the apostles and the seven chosen men? Here we go:
"So God's message continued to spread. The number of believers greatly increased in Jerusalem, and many of the Jewish priests were converted, too." (Acts 6:7).

What a testimony! Not only did the message continue to spread and the number of believers increase, but Jewish priests (leaders) were even converted. I believe this was a direct consequence of the apostles' mature leadership. As they demonstrated real care, appointed specialised leadership to handle the practical issues at hand, focused on their calling, practiced mutual accountability and functioned in an exemplary way as a diverse team, they levelled the ground for delightful fruit to grow.

But what sets the apostles apart from most contemporary leadership teams is the fact that they had a mutual understanding of who their ultimate leader was:

The one true King.

Chapter 5

Who's Our Centre?

My sabbatical was about to end, and I became increasingly nervous. I wasn't planning on going back to the way things were before; I knew that this wouldn't work for me anymore. I was also convinced that a team leadership approach - much like the apostles modelled - would be a lot more fruitful for the team and for the Base at large. I was hoping that now, four years after my first attempt, the team would be ready to embrace such a change. But what if they weren't?

When I returned to the Base after my sabbatical, we arranged re-entry coaching for our leadership team with an experienced coach. While debriefing the team about the past four months, the coach asked: "So how did it go during Bruno's absence?" Without mentioning too many details about their response, it basically became clear that the team had coped very well. They had discovered new aspects of leadership; were confronted with expectations of people to an extent they hadn't experienced before; and most of all, they had grown in their personal leadership and in confidence. Their new experience of having to carry the final responsibility without any backup, was a good one, though not necessarily easy.

I was greatly blessed as I listened to them sharing, and on several occasions I had tears in my eyes as the team members expressed empathy and a deeper understanding of the challenges I had experienced as the overall leader. Through their sharing, I realised that we were closer than ever to the change which I had anticipated for so long.

During this debriefing process, one of the team members shared a very interesting experience. He recalled a particular leadership meeting during which the team had a difficult issue to address. Literally hours of discussion and processing went into this matter that morning, without any satisfactory outcome. When they still couldn't find a solution and were starting to get tired, someone in the team suggested: "Maybe we should give Bruno a call. Surely he will know what to do." However, the team quickly agreed that this wasn't an option, as they had committed to not disturb me during my sabbatical.

Maybe we should pray and ask the Lord for a solution?

Eventually someone else proposed: "Maybe we should pray and ask the Lord for a solution?", which the team duly did.

Within minutes they received a great solution from the Lord of how to solve the problem at hand; a solution they were not able to produce before, despite the hours of discussion.

Our coach skilfully perceived the need to unpack this particular experience and continued with an illustration. He took some of the water glasses that were standing on our table and formed a circle with them, explaining that each glass represented a member of the leadership team. He then took one more glass and said that this final glass represented me.

The coach then asked: "If this circle represents your leadership team, and you think back to the moment when some wanted to call Bruno for a solution, where did you position Bruno?" You could have heard a penny drop, because although everyone knew the answer, it was one of those answers which would cause you to feel exposed if you had to speak it out. But after a while someone graciously responded: "We positioned him in the centre of the circle."

Where did you position Bruno?

The coach smiled as he placed "my" glass right in the centre of the circle which he had formed with the other glasses. It wasn't a vicious or devaluing kind of smile, rather it was a smile that seemed to say: "I am pleased to have witnessed your insight and humility".

Immediately, the coach asked a follow-up question: "And who did you end up bringing into the centre when you eventually prayed?" All of us responded in unison and with conviction: "Jesus!"

A great silence followed as we allowed this revelation to sink in. We all knew that this example clearly illustrated the reality of our leadership dynamic over the past few years. It was more comfortable and seemingly faster to just place Bruno, instead of Jesus, in the centre of our decision making. But I realised that it wasn't just the team who had put me there, I had also allowed this to happen. Maybe I had even sought after it to some extent, although not consciously. The truth was that in some way I actually enjoyed being in the centre. It gave me a sense of importance and of being needed. And although I'm not someone who particularly strives for power, it did give me a sense of power and I did enjoy the convenience and prominence that accompanied this leadership dynamic.

Ironically, it was this very same "big boss" dynamic that had also been my greatest leadership struggle: the fact that no-one would accept a "yes" or a "no", unless the "big boss" had given it himself. This "big boss" was me and yet I knew that the burden that came with it was too big for me to carry alone. In some ways I became the people's messiah - similar to what Moses or the kings unintentionally had become to the Israelites. Having a king can become really comfortable as it releases individuals from any responsibility. But it also comes at a great cost, as God had warned the Israelites through Samuel (see 1 Samuel 8). In the same way, being a king too has its comforts but also its pains.

As we discovered in the second chapter of this book, God never intended for us to be kings nor to have kings rule over us. Instead He created us to co-rule with Him, the one true King, out of an intimate and trusting relationship with Him. Our coach had pointed this out to us in such a discerning way that we all had to simply embrace it.

> **He created us to co-rule with Him, the one true King.**

It didn't seem like we needed more explanation. We were convicted and understood that we needed to make changes. Yet the coach continued and what he shared with us next came as an unexpected confirmation of what God had already shared with us before. To our surprise the coach quoted to us the verses from Acts 6:1-7. He didn't know that God had already spoken to us through this portion of Scripture. God used our coach to not only remind us of His word to us, but now also to give us a deeper understanding and revelation of what this Scripture could mean in our context. We started to see much clearer how this apostolic leadership model could be applied in our context: how it could empower many others while at the same time releasing us as a leadership team to spend more time with the Lord, putting Him in the centre, hearing Him together and in that way co-leading with Him in a team context.

Of course we still had lots of questions about how such team leadership, where God and not man was in the centre, would look in practice. We were so used to having one leader that it was a huge paradigm shift to transition to imagining a team without an overall human leader. We didn't know exactly how this would work, but we now had the conviction and the faith that it could work since it had also worked for the apostles. Some of our initial questions were no different from those we were later asked by others when we started to introduce our new model to them. I will try to answer some of the most frequent and relevant questions later in Chapter 9 - Common Questions.

Towards the end of our debriefing retreat we decided together that we would try this Jesus-centred leadership model. We were in complete unity about it! This doesn't mean that we weren't insecure about how this would eventually play out, but we all agreed that it was worth a try since we all saw the need for change.

> **We were in complete unity about it!**

We did acknowledge that this transition wouldn't be easy and that we might tend to default back to our comfort zone of the one-man-leadership patterns, which we'd known and functioned under all our lives. As we shared this and other concerns openly with each other, we found the willingness to extend grace to one another if we were to fall back into old patterns, and to practice loving accountability in the season ahead of us. We knew that if we wanted to succeed in this process we would have to help each other.

And so we decided, in April 2017, that for the following few months we would try a team leadership model where Jesus would be the centre and our leader, and where together we would seek Him and listen to Him. We would seek consensus on what we believed to have heard from the Lord and then lead the Base together out of the strength of such unity.

At this stage, we felt comfortable to apply this new approach within our leadership team without yet announcing it to our staff body, so that if it failed for some reason, we could easily revert back to the previous model of leadership without too much disruption to our staff. What followed was a few months of exploring and growing. Of course we did experience some difficulties and challenges, but overall it started to work very well for us and we all grew to really like this new, yet ancient way. Soon we would be ready to present this leadership model to all our staff.

Chapter 6

A Sneak Peek

I'm now taking you to one of my favourite Bible discoveries. The Book of Acts blesses us with quite detailed "minutes" of three meetings (or gatherings) of the apostles. One of them we've already unpacked when we looked at Acts 6:1-7 in earlier chapters. Let us now take a sneak peek of the other two meetings and explore some useful principles on how the apostles wrestled for answers and how they found and formed them as they modelled Jesus-centred team leadership.

In Acts 1, Luke gives account of a meeting that happened soon after the ascension of Christ. The apostles, together with about 120 other believers, were gathered for prayer in the upper room of the house they were staying in. Verses 13-15 provides a rough attendance register of all the people who were present. It lists all 11 apostles by name, the mother and brothers of Jesus and several other women. It then mentions that a total of about 120 believers were gathered in one place when Peter stood up and addressed them. He started by sharing how *"the Scripture had to be fulfilled concerning Judas".* (Acts 1:16). Judas Iscariot, who used to be one of the 12 apostles until he betrayed Jesus and later died, had to be replaced. Peter received this revelation from the Lord through two passages in the book of Psalms where Judas' fate and the consequent required action was already predicted by the Holy Spirit through King David.

Peter carried a substantial leadership role in the early church, but even so, he was not exclusively making all the decisions. The fact that Peter stood up here and addressed the believers, therefore, didn't make him the leader, senior pastor or head-apostle. Peter simply had a revelation from the Lord as he was united in prayer with all the other believers. This revelation compelled him to stand up and address the others, not because of his position, but because he was the one who "happened" to receive the revelation. And what Peter shared was well received. Again, not because of his position, but because of Peter's spiritual authority and because what he shared was a God inspired revelation.

> **The fact that Peter stood up here and addressed the believers, therefore, didn't make him the leader, senior pastor or head-apostle.**

Peter then went on and proposed:
21 "So now we must choose a replacement for Judas from among the men who were with us the entire time we were traveling with the Lord Jesus— 22 from the time he was baptized by John until the day he was

taken from us. Whoever is chosen will join us as a witness of Jesus' resurrection." (Acts 1:21-22).

Apart from his initial revelation that a replacement for Judas was required, Peter also received Divine wisdom as to the criteria for such a replacement: *"men who were with us the entire time we were traveling with the Lord Jesus— from the time he was baptized by John until the day he was taken from us…"* and they needed to be *"a witness of Jesus' resurrection."* (Acts 1:22).

Based on this criteria the believers present nominated two men:
"23 …Joseph called Barsabbas (also known as Justus) and Matthias." 24 Then they all prayed, 'O Lord, you know every heart. Show us which of these men you have chosen 25 as an apostle to replace Judas in this ministry, for he has deserted us and gone where he belongs.' 26 Then they cast lots, and Matthias was selected to become an apostle with the other eleven." (Acts 1:23-26).

Let me paraphrase this story to bring more clarity: Peter had a revelation from the Lord. He stood up and shared it with the believers. He proposed that they should choose a man to replace Judas and become one of the 12 apostles. After running the possible nominees against the criteria that Peter had laid out, the believers submitted two nominations. Doubtlessly both of the nominees would have been excellent apostles, as they had met the said criteria, but because there was only one available space among them, a choice had to be made. Instead of a democratic election process, the believers prayed and asked the Lord to choose the right one. And then something really interesting happened: they cast lots. "Wait a minute," you may ask, "are you saying the way the believers tried to hear the Lord's voice was by casting lots?" Well, yes, that's exactly what I'm saying, based on how I read this passage. The believers knew that both candidates were a match, it didn't really matter to them which one would be the new apostle, but they trusted that in casting lots, God would be the One choosing the right individual in His eyes. And so it was.

Somewhat of a freeing approach, isn't it? But I think it is important to take note that they didn't cast lots out of insecurity or an unwillingness to make decisions. Instead they cast lots out of deep faith in the Lord, after they had done their diligent homework. They had looked at the criteria and adhered to them. Only then they prayerfully invited the Lord to make the final decision. It is a marvellous example of co-leading with the Lord. Everyone engages and contributes while Jesus is kept at the centre.

> **Instead they cast lots out of deep faith in the Lord, after they had done their diligent homework.**

The second recorded meeting of the apostles, elders and some of the believers is as remarkable as this one. The circumstances are totally different though, plus this time it is not Peter convening the meeting, but James. We can find the "minutes" of this meeting in Acts 15.

And here's the context: Paul and Barnabas were in Antioch, Syria, and strongly disagreed with some men who were teaching the believers that unless they were circumcised as per the requirement of the law of Moses, they could not be saved. This caused quite a bit of discussion in the local church and so it was decided that Paul and Barnabas, accompanied by some local believers, would travel to Jerusalem to seek counsel from the apostles and elders regarding this disagreement. And off they went. Now, let us read what happened next:

4 When they arrived in Jerusalem, Barnabas and Paul were welcomed by the whole church, including the apostles and elders. They reported everything God had done through them. 5 But then some of the believers who belonged to the sect of the Pharisees stood up and insisted, "The Gentile converts must be circumcised and required to follow the law of Moses."
6 So the apostles and elders met together to resolve this issue. 7 At the meeting, after a long discussion, Peter stood and addressed them as follows: "Brothers, you all know that God chose me from among you some time ago to preach to the Gentiles so that they could hear the Good News and believe. 8 God knows people's hearts, and he confirmed that he accepts Gentiles by giving them the Holy Spirit, just as he did to us. 9 He made no distinction between us and them, for he cleansed their hearts through faith. 10 So why are you now challenging God by burdening the Gentile believers with a yoke that neither we nor our ancestors were able to bear? 11 We believe that we are all saved the same way, by the undeserved grace of the Lord Jesus." (Acts 15:4-11).

So here's Peter again. This time he's not convening the meeting though. Instead, he is presenting his argument concerning the dispute at hand. Peter had quite some experience, remember? In Acts 10, we read about how God called Peter to reach out to the Gentiles for the first time. And when he did, the Holy Spirit took over and *"fell upon all who were listening"* to Peter's message (Acts 10:44). At first, this account was not received well by the other apostles and believers, but after Peter had testified in detail about what had happened, *"they stopped objecting and began praising God. They said, 'We can see that God has also given the Gentiles the privilege of repenting of their sins and receiving eternal life.'"* (Acts 11:18b).

It made total sense for Peter to stand up and defend the Gentiles' position as he himself had not initially believed that Gentiles could be saved, until the Lord taught him otherwise. Peter had to share his experience in this field, and it became a vital contribution in resolving the dispute at hand.

After Peter, it was Barnabas' and Paul's turn to share their own experience of how God had done miraculous signs and wonders among the Gentiles through them. I can literally picture the discussions among the apostles, elders and believers that were present. Some were vehemently fighting for their legalistic conviction that the Gentiles would have to obey the letter of the Law, while others passionately shared their experience of how God had freed the Gentiles and given them eternal life through Jesus.

13 When they had finished, James stood and said, "Brothers, listen to me. 14 Peter has told you about the time God first visited the Gentiles to take from them a people for himself. 15 And this conversion of

Gentiles is exactly what the prophets predicted. As it is written...". (Acts 15:13-15).

> **Nowhere does it say that James was the overall leader of the apostles.**

Again, I find this an appealing example of leadership. Nowhere does it say that James was the overall leader of the apostles. They were a team, where Jesus was kept in the centre. But this didn't stop James from taking leadership in this tense situation, and everyone seemed happy with him doing so. Disputes and discussions like this often need some form of leadership. But this leadership couldn't possibly have been taken on by Peter. He wouldn't have been objective as he clearly sided with the Gentiles. James had the anointing for the moment. He had the grace to patiently and carefully listen to everyone before he stood up. But he also got a special revelation from the Lord, as he was reminded of what the prophets had predicted, and so he shared this revelation with everyone. This then led him to the following conclusion:

19 "And so my judgment is that we should not make it difficult for the Gentiles who are turning to God. 20 Instead, we should write and tell them to abstain from eating food offered to idols, from sexual immorality, from eating the meat of strangled animals, and from consuming blood. 21 For these laws of Moses have been preached in Jewish synagogues in every city on every Sabbath for many generations." (Acts 15:19-21).

James had the boldness to announce his judgment. A judgment that was well grounded in the experience of Peter, Barnabas and Paul, but also in Scripture. And so it came to pass that the apostles and elders agreed with James' verdict. Together with the whole church in Jerusalem, they chose delegates to go with Paul and Barnabas back to Antioch to convey this decision. They were given a letter to take along in which the apostles and elders explained the decision that had been made and encouraged the church of Antioch (see Acts 15:22-27).

There's one passage in the letter which I really enjoy. To announce the decision that had been made, they wrote:

28 "For it seemed good to the Holy Spirit and to us to lay no greater burden on you [the Gentiles] than these few requirements: 29 You must abstain from eating food offered to idols, from consuming blood or the meat of strangled animals, and from sexual immorality. If you do this, you will do well. Farewell." (Acts 15:28-29).

It seemed good to the Holy Spirit and to us.

They didn't use phrases like "thus says the Lord" or "this is our decision and it cannot be challenged". Instead they made this humble statement: *"It seemed good to the Holy Spirit and to us"*. (verse 28). Isn't that a lovely way of communicating their decision? And it beautifully reflects, yet again, what it means to co-lead with God. Engaging, applying wisdom, trusting for revelation, stepping out in faith, while keeping Him at the centre.

I mentioned before that team leadership without an overall leader, doesn't mean that there should not be leadership at all. However, leadership is no longer a position but rather a calling and an anointing for a specific situation. Maybe thanks to a particular revelation from the Lord, maybe due to specialised experience, or maybe out of a trusting relationship with the people involved. Each situation might require someone else to lead. A well developed team and its members know that each situation is different and will sensitively find an appropriate and mature response. This works because they know each other well, share common values, trust each other and ultimately keep Jesus at their centre, looking to Him for wisdom and overall leadership.

Chapter 7

The Setback

During the next four months, we practiced Jesus-centred team leadership. This way of leading brought us great joy, but it also wasn't easy and the fact that I was still officially the overall leader didn't help the process.

I still felt responsible for everything, and on paper I still was. I had to learn to let go and trust the Lord, as well as the team. I had to learn to accept the team's consensus even when it differed from what I would have done if I was making the decisions alone. At the same time, I still had a valuable contribution to make, which meant I had to find a balance between letting go, yet still contributing my part.

Not only did I experience challenges in adjusting to this new way of leading, but so did the team. They had to let go of their patterns of relying on their leader and instead take up leadership when they were called on. I suppose the confusion about me still being the overall leader, yet not acting like it, must have been as much a challenge for them as it was for me. Some might have felt reluctant to express views that could offend or overrule me, knowing that I would still be the one carrying the final responsibility.

It felt almost like a dance between two partners. When dance partners are still practicing their routine, they occasionally step on each other's toes, or move in different directions when they should be perfectly synchronised with one another. Mistakes are made and a lot of effort is put into practicing their chosen routine but then, eventually, the dance is perfected and can be presented to an audience.

We too, occasionally stepped on each other's toes as we practiced this dance of team leadership. Thanks to the fact that our relationships were growing stronger and we were fairly united in our values, we managed to overcome these challenges and gradually grew into this new way of doing things. We hadn't mastered it yet, but we were steadily moving closer to the leadership model we explored in Chapter 6 - A Sneak Peek, where the apostles functioned as a team while looking to Jesus for guidance and revelation, everyone ready to step up in different situations according to their anointing, revelation, experience and relationships. As we continued to practice this style of leadership we discovered more and more of the treasures hidden in this Jesus-centred approach.

And so, it came that in September 2017, we felt ready to present our dance, this new team leadership model, to our first audience: our staff. We were confident that this model would

The Setback

work for our Base and that it would cultivate greater fruitfulness. We convened an extraordinary staff meeting to announce the new structure and give some room for the staff to process it. What we didn't sufficiently consider was the fact that although we as a team had been processing this change for months, our staff had not - at least not to the same extent that we had. To expect the staff body to process this information in one meeting, immediately agree with us and show their support, was extremely naive of us. This was however the smaller of the two mistakes we made, and it was the other, bigger, mistake that turned out to become the incubator for the toughest setback in our process.

In order to ensure that everyone would get the same message firsthand, even if they weren't able to attend this extraordinary staff meeting, we recorded a video message. Our intention in doing so was to communicate clearly and make the message available to everyone. The communication was very clear indeed. There was little room for anyone to misunderstand the concept. But here's what we did wrong and what accounted for the bigger of our two mistakes: I was the one delivering the message on the video, and I basically did it on my own! None of us team members consciously noticed this fact nor considered this to be a concern.

> **Unfortunately, even after having practiced team leadership for a few months, we hadn't understood the value of also communicating as a team.**

Unfortunately, even after having practiced team leadership for a few months, we hadn't yet understood the value of also communicating as a team. Instead we communicated a new team-focused model in a top-down approach: The top leader made the announcement and that's the way things would be. I even used phrases such as "we are going to...", "we will..." and the likes. It was a very directive approach: A message from a director to his staff which really should have been a family conversation between elders and members of the family. We introduced a new concept by modelling the exact opposite.

> **We introduced a new concept by modelling the exact opposite.**

We shouldn't have been surprised that this approach didn't achieve our desired outcome. But we genuinely were. Instead of processing the content of my message, the staff used the time given as a platform to vent their accumulated frustration and mistrust in leadership. And it didn't stop after this meeting. Over the next few days and weeks these expressed frustrations developed into such extensive issues that we had to invite mediators to come alongside us in this process. These mediators skilfully and tirelessly helped us to unpack the issues underlying these frustrations and mistrust, and to process them well by sharing, listening and forgiving one another. Together we started a process of restoring trust between our staff and the leadership, but also between different staff groupings. It took us nearly 18 months to go through the full extent of this mediation procedure.

The Setback

For many of us it was a very painful process and it left us with some scars. That said, it was absolutely imperative for us to go through this process if we wanted this envisioned Jesus-centred team leadership to have a feasible chance. We all had an immense need to mature and to grow in our communication skills, in understanding others and in godly leadership principles. We needed to step towards one another and learn to trust each other. This process, albeit a painful one, helped replace some of our shaky foundations with rock solid material, which would be safe to build on.

Unfortunately, this process did not remain a matter of internal affairs. False rumours quickly spread into the whole region of YWAM Southern Africa, and all of a sudden our leadership team didn't just face internal challenges but also blazing arrows of attack from the outside. My leadership of the past years was questioned and challenged, and I had to constantly keep my heart in check, forgiving and releasing those who had so wrongfully judged me.

At the same time our team came under attack from various sides. Some judged us based on rumours; others expressed doubts about whether team leadership, the way we envisioned it, would work; and still others suggested that we should all step down and allow a new leader to come take over and lead our ministry into success. These attacks came from all sorts of people. People inside and outside our Mission, people in leadership and people without any leadership responsibilities. Just like the spectators of a soccer World Cup Final, everyone knew best what had to happen, but only a few people really seemed to genuinely care and offer their sincere, loving and compassionate help. But by God's grace, those few were there.

This was a tough setback. In fact, I have tears in my eyes as I write this and recall some of the heartache that I experienced during this time. And I know that many of our team members experienced a pain comparable to mine during this process. It was a difficult time for all of us. While the pain was real, and caused to a great extent by unfair treatment, it did not take away the fact that without going through this process, we would have lost so much more than the comfort of a pain free leadership.

> **This was a tough setback.**

The grievances our staff expressed weren't so much about us moving to a team leadership structure and not having one overall leader anymore, but rather they were about a lack of trust, a lack of timely communication and also about cultural differences. These issues had to be addressed before we could move forward with a change to our leadership structure, as the team leadership model requires a high level of trust, healthy communication as well as mutual values.

In retrospect, we realised that it was God's grace that allowed these issues to surface, so that we could address and respond to them with the help of our mediators.

The Setback

2019 became the year of new beginnings. A year when the Lord gave our Base fresh and renewed vision, when we intentionally built trust with the staff body and when we all (re-)discovered our individual roles - our personal puzzle piece - in the bigger picture of YWAM Worcester. We didn't live without challenges, disputes or arguments, but we learned to handle these better, assume the best of one another and to again take the risk to trust each other. It was a year of regaining confidence, trust, joy and vision. It was also a year when we started to practice team leadership on our Base beyond the scope of our Base leadership team. More and more we all learned to appreciate and embrace a leadership model where Jesus is held at the centre.

We were closer than ever before, but one step was still missing: The official stepping down of the overall leader, me, and the inauguration of a leadership team of equals with Jesus at the centre. And as we wait for God to show us the right timing for this step, we continue to practice keeping Him at the centre of our team, as we lead.

Chapter 8

Conflict Resolution

One of the problems that surfaced during our mediation process was the fact that most people on our Base - students, staff and leadership alike - did not practice a godly way of resolving disputes with one another. Most of us either avoided conflict completely, went behind the offender's back and caused rumours and gossip, or expected a third party (preferably someone in leadership) to intervene and address the issue with the offender. Others of us didn't necessarily avoid conflict, but lacked the skills to address issues with the necessary love and compassion.

When our mediators observed this problem amongst us, they gave us a crash course on the Matthew 18 principle. As we meditated on this passage, we soon recognised the need for us to master the principle contained in it if we wanted to be a community that modelled Christlikeness.

I'm using the Message translation to quote this portion of Scripture, as I find it draws out the underlying value of it so exquisitely:

"If a fellow believer hurts you, go and tell him—work it out between the two of you. If he listens, you've made a friend. If he won't listen, take one or two others along so that the presence of witnesses will keep things honest, and try again. If he still won't listen, tell the church. If he won't listen to the church, you'll have to start over from scratch, confront him with the need for repentance, and offer again God's forgiving love." (Matthew 18:15-17 - MSG).

In this passage, Jesus speaks to His disciples and the first thing Jesus points out is that if there is an issue between you and someone else, it is to be addressed in private, just between you and them. It's not something you first share with your best friend, your spouse or your prayer group. It's a matter between you and them. You address it, in love, and chances are that *"he listens"* and *"you've made a friend"*.

> **...if there is an issue between you and someone else, it is to be addressed in private, just between you and them.**

Does this principle only apply if a *"fellow believer"* hurts you? I don't think so. Whenever you witness (or think you witness) someone doing something wrong, hurtful, sinful or harmful, this passage of Scripture calls you to address it with the said person on a one-on-one basis. Of course there's wisdom to be applied here too. If you need to address something with a child, you had best draw his parents in. If you need to address something with a person of the opposite sex, it might be wise to draw in one of their trusted friends or their spouse. The point is that we should not avoid conflict and start gossip, but rather we should reach out to the person so that we may help them and *"win a friend"*.

It's also important to note that sometimes we witness something and come to our own conclusions based on our assumptions. We must understand that we can often perceive a situation wrongly since we usually don't have the full picture. A situation or action may look clearly wrong to us, but if we were to understand the context, the situation or action might appear very different. Let me illustrate this point with a funny experience that I had.

One day, I was a guest at a wedding of friends. Together with some of the other guests, we planned a prank to hijack the bride and whisk her away on a bicycle carriage. Traditionally, the groom was then expected to search for his missing bride. I was the designated hijacker and accordingly dressed up like a groom. When the real groom was distracted, I "captured" his newly wedded wife, asked her to sit on the nicely prepared carriage and then drove away with her. The carriage was decorated with a poster that said "Just Married" and as we were cruising along the lake promenade, strangers were congratulating and celebrating us because they assumed that I was the rightful bridegroom. But I wasn't. In the eyes of the onlookers, the circumstances appeared to be clear: A newly married couple was cruising around on a bicycle carriage. But the people who were strolling along the promenade that day did not have the bigger context of the story and therefore came to the wrong conclusion based on their assumptions. I wasn't the bridegroom and therefore they were wrong in their interpretation of the events they saw. But not to worry, the rightful bridegroom did eventually pursue us and conquer the evil hijacker to win his bride back. (Did I just refer to myself as "evil"?)

This lighthearted story simply illustrates that we can easily perceive something to be true, when our perception is in fact very far from the truth. And that's why we should never pass a quick judgement but rather seek conversation, at least if we sincerely care about the other person's wellbeing.

We can easily perceive something to be true, when our perception is in fact very far from the truth.

In the diverse cross-cultural context of our YWAM community there is perpetual room for misinterpretation, misunderstanding and misjudgment. Someone does or says something with the best intention, not knowing that in another person's culture this very thing is perceived as offensive or maybe even sinful. To avoid unintentional offence and misjudgment it is therefore advisable to always ask questions, in order to understand why a person did or said something and what the heart behind it was. In most cases, we may find that the person's intentions were not bad. Instead there may be a need for them (and/or me) to learn more about the other culture(s) around them so that they can interact better with others.

Unfortunately, it is much more comfortable for us not to confront a person who has offended us. It is easy to find all kinds of excuses like: "What if I end up offending the person in return? What if the person attacks me? What if I was wrong? What if I don't find the right words? What if...?"

Loving confrontation is a skill that can be learnt, and needs to be learnt, if we are followers of Christ. We are not responsible for the other person's response, but we are responsible for our own actions and words, and our own attempt to *"make a friend"*. The heart behind addressing a situation with another person should always be to clarify, and if necessary to disciple the person in a win-back-over type of way. We should all practice this kind of loving confrontation on an ongoing basis.

> **Loving confrontation is a skill that can be learnt.**

In the unlikely, but possible event that the person doesn't respond well to your loving confrontation, Jesus suggests that you should *"take one or two others along so that the presence of witnesses will keep things honest, and try again."* Careful here: Jesus doesn't say "go to one or two others and share with them how horrible the other person is". He also doesn't suggest going to one or two others and asking them to go address the offender on your behalf. Jesus suggests taking one or two others along. This means you go, together with one or two witnesses, and you try again. It is your responsibility to address the offender and you cannot just hand it over to someone else. This approach is a compelling way of protecting your relationship with the person who offended you. It is so easy for an offence to fester between two people. Jesus' approach requires you to put measures in place in order to prevent the issue from escalating into something it is not, thus protecting your relationship. Accompanied by witnesses to keep things honest, you may have won a friend back. Still not the case?

Well, then Jesus encourages you to take it a step further: *"If he still won't listen, tell the church."* Who is the church? The Greek word used here for church is "ekklésia", which means: "...a company of Christians, or of those who, hoping for eternal salvation through Jesus Christ, observe their own religious rites, hold their own religious meetings, and manage their own affairs, according to regulations prescribed for the body for order's sake. Those who anywhere, in a city, village, constitute such a company and are united into one body..." (Strong's Concordance).

It is therefore the Christian community that we're a part of that should keep us accountable for our actions towards one another. Therefore, the next step in the process described in Matthew 18 would be to take the person who offended you to the local group of believers that you're a part of, and to address the issue with them. Practically, this could be done by consulting with the leadership of the community which you're a part of. The leadership will ideally ensure that all the previous processes have been followed well, all the facts are verified and all has been done with the best intentions and the other person's best interest at heart. If the offence still can't be resolved, then it might be that the offender does not share the same values that you do. That's why Jesus then says: *"you'll have to start over from scratch, confront him with the need for repentance, and offer again God's forgiving love."* Or as we read in the NLT translation: *"Then if he or she won't accept the church's decision, treat that person as a pagan or a corrupt tax collector."*

Now, how exactly did Jesus treat the pagan and the corrupt tax collector? Hint: think of Zacchaeus, the chief tax collector of Jericho, whom Jesus visited for a meal. It seems that the sheer presence of Jesus led Zacchaeus' to repentance. (Luke 19:1-10).

Treating someone like a corrupt tax collector doesn't mean we chase them to hell, as is sometimes believed. Indeed, we might exclude them from our fellowship or community if the offence is significant enough and they don't share our values, but we should still maintain an honest and caring heart which desires to win them back over, in much the same way as we are called to have a caring heart towards anyone who still needs to learn about the need for repentance and about God's forgiving love. Yes, clear boundaries may be needed, but at the same time we should never lose compassion for our fellow believers, even if they have offended us.

> **Treating someone like a corrupt tax collector doesn't mean we chase them to hell.**

The passage which we've just explored in Matthew 18:15-17, is shortly followed by Peter asking Jesus: *"Master, how many times do I forgive a brother or sister who hurts me? Seven?"* and Jesus replied, *"Seven! Hardly. Try seventy times seven."*
(Matthew 18:21-22 - MSG).

Generous forgiveness towards someone who has offended us is a vital and foundational part of this process of loving confrontation. It means that forgiveness is inseparable from this act of discipleship.

As our leadership team delved into this Matthew 18 principle, our relationships with one another started to deepen and we began to trust one another more. Of course it would be wrong to claim that we became masters of this skill overnight, but our awareness grew, and is still growing, steadily. As issues and situations surface we remember more often than not to apply this newly learnt principle, and we hold one another accountable to apply this principle. At times we have to disciple individuals who are hoping to pass their responsibility on to us by asking us to intervene on their behalf. In these cases, we've learnt to lovingly pass the responsibility back to the person again.

It's not always straightforward to recognise how this principle applies in a given situation, and we may find that we can't always apply the steps precisely as laid out in Matthew 18. But when we get a hold of the heart of this Scripture, and perceive the value of it, it allows us to adapt and find creative solutions where needed. Matthew 18:15-17 has become one of the keys in our Community as we learn to live more harmoniously with each other in this diverse cross-cultural context we find ourselves in. It is however a principle that needs to be intentionally kept alive by constant reminders and ongoing teaching.

Chapter 9

Common Questions

When our leadership team initially processed this Jesus-centred team leadership approach, we asked each other, our coach and God a lot of questions.

We knew that if we wanted this new way of leading to work, we needed to at least have our major questions and concerns answered. As we wrestled with these questions we found more and more answers, but other answers were only found as we started practicing this new way of leading, and of course we are still discovering more answers as we continue our journey.

Many of the questions that we initially had, were later also asked by other individuals and groups as we processed this Jesus-centred team leadership with them. In this chapter, I wish to draft a catalogue of the most common questions people asked when confronted with this different way of leading. You might find yourself with some of the same questions, and my hope is that this chapter will help you find some sensible answers.

Of course, this list of questions and answers is in no way complete. You might also not be fully satisfied with some of the answers I offer, and that's absolutely okay. Maybe you want to take your questions to God and also process them a bit further with trusted friends, leaders and elders. It's in wrestling with these questions that deeper revelation can be found.

I'll start with one of the first questions I'm usually asked:

Who carries the final responsibility, or as they say in South Africa, "where does the buck stop" if there is no overall leader?

Well, the buck stops with us! Team leadership requires that we reach a consensus together. Once we have reached this consensus, we then execute the decision together, as a unified team. We decide who will communicate the decision and how best this should be done. (Remember how the apostles chose to communicate their decision concerning their verdict about the "Gentile issue"). We will support each other when people have questions or wrestle with our decision.

> **Well, the buck stops with us!**

Does consensus mean that the decision made is everyone's first choice?

Conflict Resolution

Contrary to popular belief, reaching a consensus does not mean that every team member supports the decision 100%, however, each team member does need to support the decision enough to commit to it.

While processing one of our more recent decisions with the entire Base, we used the following graph to help illustrate the concept of consensus.

As each team member considers the degree to which they support the decision at hand, they may either strongly agree or strongly disagree with the decision, or, most likely, will fall somewhere in between these two extremes.

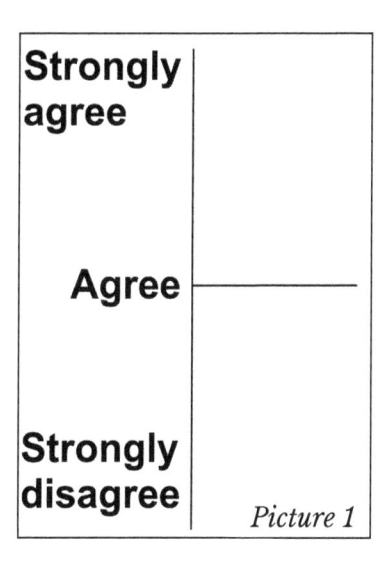

Strongly agree

Agree

Strongly disagree

Picture 1

In order to reach a consensus, everyone would need to support the decision enough to fall above the "agree" line. This "agree line" serves as a watershed and if any of the team members fall below this "agree line", a consensus has not yet been reached.

It's important to note that the scope of agreeing with a decision includes when someone has reservations about the decision and has expressed them, but chooses to trust the wisdom of the group as a whole - when it seems that the group is generally in favour of the decision.

Let me illustrate this concept with an example:

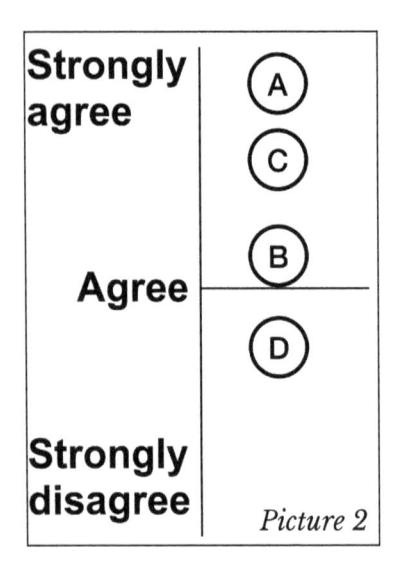

Team members A, B and C might all agree on a proposed decision, though to different degrees, while team member D might disagree with the proposal. As long as team member D disagrees, the team cannot claim a consensus. (See picture 2).

Picture 2

After further discussion, team member A might agree to some concessions, which would in turn help team member D to agree to some concessions on his end.

After these discussions and concessions, team member D might now come to the point of agreeing with the decision enough to commit to it. He still might not be excited about the decision, but he is willing and able to agree to it, due to the mutual compromise, and also due to his choosing to trust the wisdom of the team as a whole (who, as seen from the following graph, all agree on the decision). While team member A's agreement level has slightly decreased, team member B's agreement level has increased with the adjustments which now give her more peace. (Picture 3). The moment all team members have moved above the "agree line" the team has reached a consensus, even if some don't yet agree very strongly.

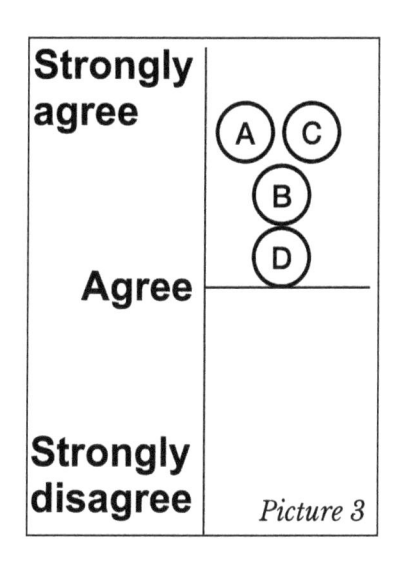

Picture 3

A consensus is only reached if every single member of the team is above the "agree line" and agrees enough with the decision to commit to it. The moment one member is below this line, the team has not yet found a consensus and therefore needs to prayerfully seek more concessions that can be agreed upon, or find a total new approach to solve the matter. The goal of a Jesus-centred team is always to find consensus as they seek the Lord's guidance together.

> **A consensus is only reached if every single member of the team is above the "agree line".**

Didn't the early church appoint bishops?

Yes, they did appoint "epískopos" (the Greek word for "overseer", from which the English word "bishop" is derived from) and "presbýteros" (Greek for elder). However, the early church most definitely had a different understanding of bishops than we do today, as our modern understanding is influenced by the historical development of church denomination structures. In the early church, the words "epískopos" and "presbýteros" were not always clearly distinguished from each other, but often used interchangeably. In Paul's letters to Timothy, he instructs him to appoint elders in Ephesus. This instruction is commonly interpreted to mean that Timothy became the overall bishop of the church of Ephesus and his role required him to appoint elders, whom he oversaw. A different interpretation is that Timothy was acting in an apostolic role, appointing elders and providing eldership to them not in an autocratic way but in an inclusive, family type of way. I'm definitely leaning towards embracing this second interpretation more as everything the apostles did, pointed towards team and not autocracy.

In our time, leaders like titles. It seems to give them a sense of security and authority. But this was not the way leadership was lived out in the times of the apostles. They did not use, need, nor rely on titles. One detail I observe in both Peter and Paul's letters seems to emphasise this very fact. We often refer to the Apostle Paul or the Apostle Peter. But both Peter and Paul generally opened their letters with the words: "Peter, an apostle of Jesus Christ" (1 Peter 1), or "This letter is from Paul, an apostle of Christ Jesus" (1 Timothy 1). By stating "an apostle of..." they are describing their calling, their function, their anointing, and not their title. If they were using "Apostle" as a title they would have introduced themselves as "Apostle Paul" or "Apostle Peter", but they didn't. The titles of bishop, apostle, pastor or even elder have developed throughout church history to emphasise authority and power. But the early church used these terms not as titles or positions but rather to describe functions and anointing that would best unfold when used under the authority of Christ and within the accountability structure of a council (team).

> **They did not use, need, nor rely on titles.**

But shouldn't we at least have a "senior among equals" who will initiate processes or finalise decisions?

Someone does indeed need to take some form of leadership to initiate processes and finalise decisions. But that someone doesn't always have to be the same person. It is much more valuable if each situation can be facilitated by someone who has authority in the said situation either through experience, relationship, interest or anointing. Throughout the Book of Acts, we can observe how the apostles had different conveners for different situations, without having appointed leaders over their team.

Doesn't it prolong decision making when a whole team needs to process every situation rather than having one leader who can make a quick decision?

Quick decisions are not always the best decisions. But yes, it often does take longer to come to a decision in a team context, as there are discussions and processes involved. However, these very processes are extremely valuable. They help us to consider a decision well and to look at it from different angles. Hearing God's voice together as a team is also a much healthier way of making decisions, rather than trying to seek God on your own as a leader. While it often takes longer to come to a decision in a team context, usually such a decision is also a more mature one - one that takes us much further as a community. The following proverb comes to my mind: "If you want to go fast, go alone. If you want to go far, go together." (African Proverb).

> **Quick decisions are not always the best decisions.**

Having said that, appropriately distributing the authority to make decisions will also help speed up the decision making process.

What about the legal requirement of having a director? Who is accountable towards the Government?

Within the South African legal framework, it is possible for an entity to have a single director, however a Board of three or more directors is preferred.

In our case, YWAM Worcester had already registered a Board of multiple directors, so no changes were needed from a legal point of view. What did need to change was our mindset, so that we would move away from the belief that one of these five directors was more important than the other four.

Even if the legislation of your country requires you to have one single director, you can still have that single director on paper for official and legal purposes, and for communications outside of your organisation, but that should not hinder you from living a Jesus-centred team leadership approach when it comes to your day-to-day internal affairs.

But isn't it dangerous if the leader lets go of their control and no one person has the final say? The organisation can easily drift from its purpose and values!

Really? Wouldn't it be easier for an organisation to drift if it is in the hands of one leader? Where there is a team, rooted in the same values and beliefs, and committed to keeping Jesus at the centre, there is little chance that the organisation will drift. In fact, a team will more likely succeed in keeping each other accountable and keeping the organisation on track.

Doesn't an organisation need one strong apostolic leader who can cast vision and lead the rest of the organisation into the fulfilment of that vision? When a team is involved, won't the team struggle to focus on one united vision?

I fully understand this concern. I've had it too. There is indeed a danger that vision could be rejected too quickly by a team if crucial elements are missing from the team dynamic. However, if the team members are 100% committed to keeping Jesus at the centre of all their decisions; if they are united in their values and if they intentionally maintain healthy relationships with one another, I see no reason for concern.

If I am a visionary, functioning in a team with these three criteria intact, then the team will embrace me for who I am, and at the same time I will embrace the other team members for who they are. I can then submit my vision to the team with confidence, knowing that they will test it against our shared values and prayerfully submit it to God. A vision that is truly divine will be confirmed by God and therefore not be turned down by the team. In fact, once a vision has been embraced in this way, it is much more likely to succeed because each of the team members have personally "bought into" the vision for themselves.

> **A vision that is truly divine will be confirmed by God and therefore not be turned down by the team.**

This is not just a theoretical idea, I have personally experienced it. In early 2019, I submitted a fresh vision for our Base to our leadership team. I had written it down in detail and drafted a mind-map to visually illustrate the vision. I was really excited as it felt like a "download straight from God". I submitted this vision to the leadership team and asked them to prayerfully consider it. Some of the team members were literally alarmed by the extent of the vision and what it would mean for us, and certainly the vision was inviting us to a reality that was rather different from the one we were currently experiencing. But despite their fear, they committed to seek the Lord and hear from Him. And so it came that the Lord confirmed it to each member of the team. There was even a sense of excitement and anticipation which eventually spilled over to the whole Base when we processed it with our staff. When I experienced this, it gave me great peace that Jesus-centred team leadership would totally be capable of embracing and promoting vision. As a matter of fact, a leadership team would even be more likely to embrace additional visions, beyond those of the one visionary leader. What an enrichment would that be!?

Do you suggest that this leadership model should be adopted by everyone in leadership?

Although I do believe this model of Jesus-centred team leadership is "A More Desirable Way" of leadership, I do not suggest that everyone by default should change the way they are leading. In this book, I'm simply sharing about how God has led us at YWAM Worcester, and some of the things we've learned so far on this journey. I don't know your situation and what exactly God has in mind for you. But the great thing is that you can ask Him! The key lies in the relationship we have with God. He is the one who knows what is best for you and your situation. So my encouragement to everyone at any time is always: "What is the Lord saying to you?" - then follow His advice and lead in obedience without compromising. And you can be sure that an exciting journey of growth will follow.

What kind of organisational structure would serve this kind of Jesus-centred leadership approach?

I don't believe that there is one optimal organisational structure that would work in every situation. Depending on your current structure, your organisational culture, your size, your local context and, most importantly, what God is saying to you, your structure may look quite different from ours. I suggest that as a team you ask the Lord and process together with Him to determine what structure would best serve your organisation, and how you could best live out Jesus-centred leadership within that structure. Furthermore, I would strongly recommend that if you are making major changes to your organisational structure, you process these changes with your other leadership and staff circles in order to include everyone affected by the changes, in the process.

In transitioning from a one-man leadership model to a Jesus-centred team leadership approach, wouldn't it be easier if the previous leader just stepped down and left?

I think this is a very valid question. I've asked myself this question several times, and sometimes I've even asked our team whether it wouldn't be better for me to leave. Again, there's probably no generic answer that applies to everyone. There might be situations where it would be easier for a team to start off without the previous leader still being involved. However, if the transition is managed in a fairly healthy way, then I see much value in the previous leader staying involved to some extent, being available with their expertise, their anointing and their care. This approach would however require a leader who does not have a tendency to want to control and is comfortable with letting go of their power. It also requires team members who are not easily threatened or intimidated by a possibly strong personality, and are confident to step up and lead when their anointing is called for.

Where can we see this leadership approach modelled?

As helpful as it would be, I didn't find many examples of team based leadership without a main leader, and even less so Jesus-centred team leadership. However, these models do exist, they're just not easy to find.

- **In the business world** there is a model called Holacracy (and there are other similar models too). Although this is not particularly a Jesus-centred model, it could, embraced by Christian business people, most definitely be adapted to such. Instead of structuring an organisation with a top-down management hierarchy, the Holacracy model decentralises the management of an organisation by distributing the authority and decision making powers to self-organised teams. These teams have a clearly expressed scope of authority and can make decisions that fall within their scope.

- **In government**, the closest to a team based leadership model that I could think of is that of the Swiss Presidency. Switzerland actually doesn't have one single president, but rather, a Federal Council. This Federal Council consists of seven members and forms the executive government of the Swiss Confederation. Each year, a different member of the Federal Council acts as the Swiss President, and at the end of every year the role rotates to another of the members. The role of president requires a member to convene meetings and represent the Federal Council internationally, but it does not have the unilateral power that most presidents of other countries would have. Now, as much as this is a beautiful model of team leadership, it does not model Jesus-centredness.

- **In the sphere of the church**, according to my experience, we find a handful of YWAM Bases, other organisations and churches around the world that are practicing Jesus-centred team leadership. But I believe the best model we can find is still the one of the apostles, as described in the Book of Acts.

Could I implement Jesus-centred team leadership in a business context too, or does it only work in a church or missions context?

If a team is following Jesus and commits to putting Him at the centre of their dealings and decisions, then it is my conviction that this model will work in any context. There might be small adaptations needed, but this model isn't a static way of doing things anyway, and is therefore capable of being tailored to a particular setting. I believe a business will greatly benefit from a team that leads together while keeping Jesus at the centre. And as we saw in the previous answer, there are already leadership models applied in the business sphere that could easily be adjusted to a Jesus-centred approach. I'm sure that as you explore this option in prayer, the Lord will gladly guide you on such a journey. So why not ask Him to find out if this may be something for you and your business?

Chapter 10

A More Desirable Way

You might have more questions than what I could address in the previous chapter. I encourage you, once again, to take your questions to the Lord, seeking Him for answers and allowing Him to speak into your unique situation. He has an opinion, He has a plan, and most of all, He loves to co-create with you. Wrestling with your questions won't necessarily be easy, but chances are good that it will be extremely enriching.

Although I still haven't found the answers to all my questions, for me this kind of leadership has definitely become "A More Desirable Way". I have observed how this approach has drawn us much closer together as a team. Together, we are more aware of our need to depend on God and we more frequently seek His presence to hear from Him so that we can obediently build on the Word of the Lord for us.

I am convinced that it is essential to pursue the following three qualities as we seek to apply this "More Desirable Way" of team leadership:

1. **Jesus at the centre**

A commitment from everyone on the team to keep Jesus at the centre and to keep each other accountable in this regard. Prayer and hearing His voice need to be practiced regularly - both corporately as a team and individually.

2. **Mutual values**

As much as possible the team needs to agree on their values and beliefs, and commit to keeping them alive and active by discussing them with each other regularly.

3. **Healthy and trusting relationships**

The team needs to commit to working on their relationships by spending time with each other, also outside of their work context, and by lovingly addressing issues with one another quickly and in keeping with the principle laid out in Matthew 18 (see in Chapter 8 - Conflict Resolution).

A team that can consistently grow in these three foundational qualities will still not avoid mistakes and struggles, but it will most likely take the next step on this journey of the "More Desirable Way". I am certain that such a team will ultimately bring forth great fruit. In turn, it might become a catalyst for the multiplication of more such Jesus-centred leadership teams, whether smaller or larger teams, inside or outside its own organisation.

As I mentioned in the first chapter, our story at YWAM Worcester is not yet finished. We still have a process to complete and some mountains to conquer. That said, our goal isn't to reach a destination but rather to keep choosing this "More Desirable Way", and to continue engaging with the Lord in our ongoing journey.

> **That said, our goal isn't to reach a destination but rather to keep choosing this "More Desirable Way".**

With this in mind, the book you're holding isn't a complete guide to the successful implementation of this model, but rather, I hope, a valuable contribution on the journey of discovery and practice of Jesus-centred team leadership.

There's so much more that I would like to share and explore with you in light of the journey at hand. Topics such as consultative leadership, and how this is being modelled in various cultural contexts, such as in an African tribe; the strengths and giftings that should be present in a healthy team; how to intentionally build stronger relationships; exploring different structures that could facilitate the Jesus-centred team leadership approach; leadership that champions and empowers others; cross-cultural applications; and more.

But, since I'd like to keep this edition to booklet size in order to make it more appealing and accessible to busy leaders out there, these topics, as valuable they might be, will have to wait for a possible second volume to this book. This second volume could potentially even include some of the stories and testimonies gleaned from your own journey of unpacking this leadership approach? Let's see how the Lord leads.

For this edition, I hope that I have been able to share sufficient content to stir up fruitful discussions and inspire you and your team to engage with a Biblical leadership model that is not often taught in mainstream leadership books and seminars. If you too conclude that the described leadership model is "A More Desirable Way", then I wish you and your team much wisdom, patience, endurance and joy, as you discover how this model might apply in your context. May you have many Divine encounters where you find Him and His way for you and your situation.

Would you like to share your story of how God is leading you in this "More Desirable Way" of Jesus-centred team leadership? Then, I invite you to connect with me via the book's web page: www.more-desirable-way.com. I am keen to hear your testimony and learn from you, especially since I'm currently aware of only a few examples of this type of leadership in practice.

May the Lord keep on blessing you with His revelation and may you find great joy in co-creating with Him:

The one true King!

The Crown

On this final page, I invite you to take a moment to observe the symbol of the crown that has accompanied you on your journey through this book.

Can you see Jesus at the centre, holding the hands of the team members around Him?

As you meditate on this image, what else do you feel the image is conveying to you?

ShareOne®

Like what you've read? Why not share this book with someone else!

This book is not a money-making project, and so I have decided that instead of receiving royalties from the sales of this book, I will re-invest potential profits back into my passion of encouraging others who too are longing for a different, "More Desirable Way" of leadership.

By buying this book, you too are contributing to this work of stirring, empowering and equipping others who desire to lead differently. All profits, beyond the cost of printing and administration, will go towards initiatives that support others on this journey - such as printing additional copies of this book so that we can make this book accessible to those who are financially less privileged.

This is very much also the heart of ShareOne®, my publisher: "ShareOne® lets you experience the joy of giving. That's why ShareOne® products are usually sold in packs of two. One product you keep for your own use and the other one you give away as a gift. Generosity's fun! Give it a try!"

If you too want to ShareOne® of this book with someone else, simply buy another copy and bless someone you know or visit www.more-desirable-way.com where you can give a book to someone by means of a financial donation.

ShareOne®
Publishings.

Pay What Feels Right

This book can be purchased at any of the major bookstores for a fixed price, as advertised by them. But I am also making this book available on www.more-desirable-way.com as a ebook-download, without a paid checkout. The idea is that you would have the freedom to choose to pay an amount that reflects what you feel this book is worth. Also, it provides room to take your economical situation into consideration. I believe in trusting others, and this is simply a way of demonstrating my trust in you. Again, the income of this book is not to make anyone rich, but to cover the administrative costs and to invest back into the work of supporting others on this journey of discovering "A More Desirable Way".

Acknowledgments

First and foremost, I want to thank God, for being my perfect Father, most understanding friend and compassionate counsellor. To Him be all the Glory!

Further, I would like to express my deep gratitude and appreciation to my team of editors, contributors, challengers and intercessors who helped shape this book into what it is, and who encouraged me when I needed it most. You are true friends! A special thank you
to Veronika Gloeck, my first editor - your incredible skills and wisdom made my English sound smart and helped me to express my heart better;
to Lauren Phillips, my second editor - your eye for the detail is such a valuable gift and highly appreciated;
to Louis Pretorius, my friend - for your prophetic and profound input and encouragement;
to Stefaan Hugo, my spiritual father - for patiently and lovingly mentoring me for so many years and for playing such a big part in shaping me into who I am today;
to Jim Stier, Lynn Green, Kobus van Niekerk, Wilson Goeda and John Mukolwe, fathers in our Mission - for sharing valuable advice and for allowing me to tap into your wealth of wisdom;

to Cliff Canipe, my friend - for giving me precious advice on the ins and outs of publishing;

and to everyone else who has in some way contributed to the successful completion of this work. You mean the world to me!

My admiration and a very special thank you goes out to the YWAM Worcester leadership team. You guys are very dear to my heart. Thank you for sticking things out with me and for your unending support and perseverance. Thank you for being patient with me during the worst of my days and for believing with me that this leadership model can work. Your pure and sincere hearts, your passion to seek the Lord and your willingness to maintain accountable relationships is a real inspiration to me! I could not wish to be part of a better team!

Whenever I think of our mission partners who have faithfully and generously supported us over the years so that we could follow the Lord's call and in this way contribute to the advancement of His Kingdom, I get goosebumps. My heart overflows with gratitude towards you all. Your prayers and gifts are deeply appreciated.

And finally, I am indebted to my awesome wife and best friend, Judy. Thank you for your genuine care, especially in times of hardship; for loving me despite my fits of pique; and for always supporting me in every aspect of my life. My deepest gratitude and love goes out to you, Darling. And to my three extraordinary kids, Noah, Joana and Yemima - thank you for always having a word of encouragement ready and for making me feel loved at all times!

About The Author

Bruno grew up in a Christian home in Switzerland and was named Loyiso by his (now late) Xhosa language teacher, Tata Jacobs. Bruno Loyiso is also a banker, musician, influencer, idealist, teacher, maximiser and dedicated family man. He obtained leadership experience as a youth group leader, orchestra and choir conductor, constable at the Swiss Army Music, pioneering leader of several church and business projects, as well as in his role as a YWAM Base leader for the past 10 years.

Bruno Loyiso has been involved with YWAM Worcester since January 2000. Together with his wife, Judy, he moved to Worcester in 2006, where the couple also became parents to a son and two daughters.